Motoring Around

SUSSEX

the first fifty years

"Let's be Jolly."

BRIGHTEN YOURSELF BY
❋ MOTOR. ❋

SMART up-to-date first-class **MOTOR CARS** about 30 per cent under London Prices may be hired from

BROWN & CO., 33, BLATCHINGTON ROAD, HOVE.

Brown & Co., Telephone No. **2,689.**

Special Private Hire Terms, INCLUDING DRIVER.

PER DAY FROM

Small Car (Voiturette) for 2 passengers (vis-a-vis) ... **2 guineas.**
Larger Car (Tonneau)   ,,   2 or 3 ,, ... 3   ,,
Large Car (Tonneau)   ,,   3 or 4 ,, ... 4   ,,

The Terms quoted are subject to alteration according to distance.   Arrangements may be made for longer or shorter periods.

☞ **ADDRESS ALL ORDERS DIRECT** to BROWN & CO., 33, Blatchington Road, Hove.
Telephone 2,689. Other communications to be sent to the Secretary at above address.

"Throw Physic to the Dogs."

The Southern Publishing Co., Ltd., 130, Church Road, Hove.—35,152.

Motoring Around

SUSSEX

the first fifty years

TIM HARDING

TEMPUS

Frontispiece: A caption is almost superfluous, except to identify the car as a *c*.1903 Darracq, and to draw attention to what seem to have been very steep hire charges.

First published 2004

Tempus Publishing Limited
The Mill, Brimscombe Port,
Stroud, Gloucestershire, GL5 2QG
www.tempus-publishing.com

British Library Cataloguing in Publication Data.
A catalogue record for this book is available from the British Library.

ISBN 0 7524 3263 X

Typesetting and origination by Tempus Publishing Limited.
Printed in Great Britain.

Contents

Acknowledgements

I have been very grateful to friends and contacts who have allowed me to use photographs from their collections, and/or provided information about pictures.

These include Peter Allen, Miss M. Burtenshaw, Mrs P. Dowser, David Fitton, David Hales, Horsham Museum, Campbell McCutcheon, Richard Mitchell, Geoff Morris, Desmond Peacock, Nic Portway, Ted Walker of Ferret Fotographics, Jeremy Wood, Mike Worthington-Williams and the Omnibus Society.

In particular, Bryan Goodman gave me the benefit of his experience in producing the companion book on Surrey, as well as a number of photographs, Alan Lambert contributed most of the bus section, Edward Reeves of Lewes provided a number of pictures from their extensive archive, and Caffyns PLC did likewise.

I apologise if I have omitted anyone else who helped, and also if I have overlooked copyright on any of the photographs reproduced.

The author's 1929 Alvis 12/50, registered PN 3306, and supplied new to Mr Harrington, of Court Lodge, Ewhurst, East Sussex.

Introduction

It is generally accepted that the arrival of the internal combustion engine, and the motor car in particular, was a mixed blessing. At the same time as opening up numerous previously inaccessible beauty spots to sightseers, the car has brought with it problems of congestion and its concomitant road development schemes which threaten that very beauty. Sussex had much to lose: not only is it near London, but its natural features have acted as a magnet to those from the Metropolis, whether as day-trippers, holidaymakers, or long-distance commuters. The car has thus had a powerful influence on the landscape as we see it today.

The county was one of the very first to witness an organised motoring event, when in November 1896 the Emancipation Run was held from London to Brighton to mark the passing of the Locomotives on Highway Act, now, of course, commemorated each year by the Veteran Car Run. Not many years later, significant speed events were held at Bexhill and Brighton, and subsequently hill-climbs at several venues, most notably South Harting. It may come as a surprise to many to realise that hill-climbs and speed trials were regularly held on unclosed public roads, such as South Harting hill, the police turning a blind eye to the proceedings. Inevitably, a serious (though not fatal) accident caused the RAC to call a halt to such events, and after April 1925 no further permits were issued. A private road across the Downs at Lewes was subsequently used up to 1939 for speed events and these attracted some notable cars and drivers. Through the 1930s the growing sport of rallying often came to Sussex: the RAC rally finished variously at Eastbourne, Hastings and Brighton, with driving tests and a Coachwork Competition.

But what of the ordinary motorist? Fortunately, the early registration records survive reasonably intact (not the case in many areas): those for the Boroughs of Brighton and Hastings are complete up to 1920, and those for the East and West divisions of the county survive in part. It is possible to establish that by the end of the first year of compulsory registration, i.e. 1904, some 1,400 vehicles had been allocated numbers by the various authorities. This is a considerable number, but it almost certainly understates the true position, as some residents would have bought their cars in London, and had them registered there.

It has been remarked on before that whereas East Sussex was the territory of the yeoman farmer, much of West Sussex comprised very large estates: Petworth, Cowdray Park, Arundel, Goodwood, Uppark and Stansted come immediately to mind. However, although to be a motorist in the early days presupposed a reasonable level of income, and although many of the landed gentry already had substantial motor-houses by this date, with cars for different purposes, a few of which are depicted here, it is obvious from some of the addresses that by no means all these early motorists and motorcyclists were moneyed. The registers are in fact a mine of information, and without them it would be hard to caption many of the photographs herein with accuracy. What are we to make of a '5 horse-power Himself (i.e. home-made) with three seats, all facing sideways' registered by Mr John Winter of 28 Montpelier Road, Brighton on 1 January 1904? Will a picture of it ever surface?

For the benefit of local historians the original two-letter registration marks issued in the county are as follows:

East Sussex AP, PM, PN, NJ
West Sussex BP, PX, PO
Brighton CD, UF
Eastbourne HC, JK
Hastings DY

The iron industry having long since departed, the Sussex of the early twentieth century was essentially rural. There were cars and motorcycles made in the county, but all were ephemeral, and none is remembered today except by the avid motor historian. Cars included the Dolphin from Shoreham, and the BPD, Lonsdale and infelicitously named Old Mill from Brighton. The Brighton records reveal several registrations of Shaw motorcycles from Crawley (the family still being actively interested in veteran machines).

More significant than these names were the coachbuilders. At a time when it was still common for the more prestigious cars to be sold as chassis, many purchasers went to a local coachworks to have a body fitted. At least four Sussex bodybuilders come to mind: Brigden of Brighton (the author owned a Delage coupé with their coachwork, and was able to hear firsthand the memories of an employee who started before the First World War), Fountain of Horsham, Harrington of Hove, and Caffyns of Eastbourne. Some of the work of the latter two firms is illustrated in this book, and the versatility of a business that could equally well body a luxury car, a lorry or a bus, is amazing.

It is the author's hope that the majority of the photographs used will be new to most readers, whether they are old car enthusiasts or local historians. Many are almost certainly published for the first time. It is hoped that they give a tantalising glimpse of what it was like to motor in Sussex during the first forty years of the last century.

More than thirty years have elapsed since the picture on page 2, and these two ladies with their Wolseley 9, snapped at Angmering-on-Sea, can drive themselves whither they please. The car, though of modest size, has special coachwork by Whittingham & Mitchel. In the background is a developer's sign, reminder of the remorseless spread of housing, partly stimulated by the car, in seaside Sussex last century.

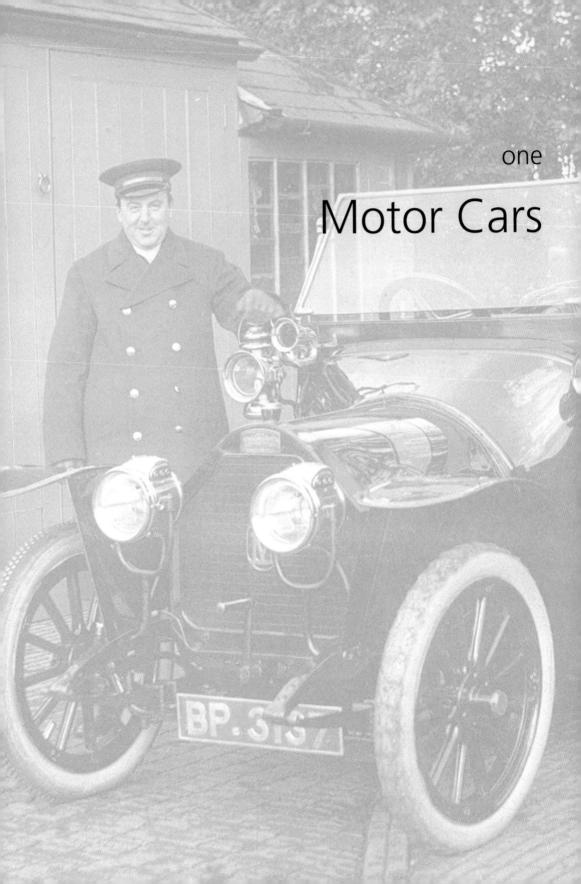

one

Motor Cars

This 10hp Daimler, with phaeton body was registered on 1 January 1904 to W. Griffiths, of New Steine, Brighton, along with five similar chassis with char-a-banc bodies. It dates however from around 1899. The combination of a heavy load and an appalling road surface must have made stopping problematic.

Carter Bros, of the Reliance Works, Billingshurst owned this curious little voiturette, believed to be a Billings with 3½hp De Dion engine. No registration number means the photograph predates 1904, and the car is probably from 1900. Note the tiller steering.

Carter Bros. also owned this 6hp Pick convertible tonneau (indicating that the rear seat was detachable) made in Stamford. The story of its demise, and of this old-established engineering works, is told in *Apprenticeship in Steam* by Jack Hampshire.

Above and below: These two photographs of racegoers leaving West Dean House for nearby Goodwood in 1903 capture well the essence of the Edwardian era. Above, driven by Mr W.D. James, and carrying the future George V as a passenger is a Gobron-Brillié, looking conventional but with an opposed-piston engine under the coal-scuttle bonnet. Below, driven by Mr Drexel, with Mrs Arthur James beside him is a 40hp Mercedes, one of the most powerful cars of its day.

BP 165 is an 8hp. Dennis tonneau of 1903, made in the adjacent county at Guildford. Dennis, of course, made their name with commercials, and buses and fire-engines in particular.

An early example of closed bodywork: BP 269 is a 10/12hp Panhard-Levassor of around 1903. Entry to the enclosed section was by a central door at the rear. The upper classes carried their crest on their cars, as they had on their carriages (see front seat).

This picture is manifestly not taken in Sussex, the Brooklands Clubhouse being visible in
the background. The car, however, is AP 107 (here seen with a trade plate 0103 AP), a 1903
Clement-Talbot 18hp rear entrance tonneau, with body by Rothschild et fils of Paris. It
was supplied new to magnate Julius Drew, of Wadhurst Hall, best known for commissioning
Lutyens to build Castle Drogo in Devon. The car survives today, having fallen into the caring
hands of the Sears family at Bolney in the 1930s, and it is a regular entrant in the London to
Brighton run. Its presence at Brooklands is probably in order to compete in a race for veteran
cars. The photograph dates from the late 1930s.

This youthful chauffeur is at the wheel of a 1903 CGV 15hp which belonged to Mr J.W.L.M.
Bretton, of Lewes. The lamps have been removed from their brackets for daytime use.

Above: The De Dion Bouton was an extremely popular and reliable light car which has survived in large numbers. Above is a 6hp model of 1903, registered BP 53. At the wheel is Mrs Nicholas Voice, and peeping from the cramped tonneau is her daughter.

Two ladies pose on a single-cylinder Darracq, CD 45, in about 1908.

Opposite below: It was not unusual for motorists to modernise their cars in order not to appear too old-fashioned: this 6hp De Dion, photographed in Worthing around 1913, when some ten years old, started life looking similar to the car above. The family look content enough even if their car was a little dated.

With a single-cylinder 6hp horizontal engine, this little Siddeley was registered in 1905: the identity of its doctor owner is unknown. This is another picture that reveals the dreadful state of the roads at that period.

Almost a twin is this 6hp Wolseley, also 1905, owned by O.R. Travers of St Leonards, since both were built at the Wolseley works. Both cars cost £175 when new.

An early Scottish-built car is this 1904 Argyll 10/12hp 2-cylinder tonneau owned by Revd J.H. Mee, whose daughter is seen at the wheel. She was the first lady to pass the ACGBI exam in driving and proficiency. Registration no. is BP 229.

From the extreme west end of the county comes this fine shot of the garages at Stansted Park, owned by the Wilder family. From left to right: Daimler, Peugeot, Rexette Tricar, Mors (in garage, and owned by H.F. Bowyer of Horndean) and Renault (owned by Claude Grahame-White, who lived at the Home Farm on the estate).

Sir Weetman Pearson was the owner of Paddockhurst, near Turners Hill. Later Lord Cowdray, his wealth is apparent from this rather faded shot of his garage. The cars include a Daimler, Mercedes, MMC, and a visiting Whitlock-Aster (AC 110).

A more modest fleet (and garage) is that of Major Gen. Campbell of Henmead Hall, Cuckfield. The tricycle is of uncertain provenance, AP 707 is a 16/20hp Cupelle tourer, and AP 261 a 12hp Clement.

SUSSEX COUNTY AUTOMOBILE CLUB.

This Club was formed in January, 1905, for the general encouragement of motoring in the County of Sussex, the discouragement of inconsiderate driving of motor vehicles, and for the convenience of motorists wanting a centre for social intercourse. The Club has 141 members. It has been instrumental in having warning boards erected in dangerous places throughout the country.

OFFICE BEARERS.

President:
MR. W. D. JAMES, West Dean Park, Chichester.

Chairman of Committee:
MR. A. SCRASE-DICKINS, Horsham.

COMMITTEE

MR. J. W. AMPS, Uckfield	Capt. F. D. LYON, Brighton
MR. J. CANNINGTON, Brighton	MR. E. E. MILLER, Patcham
MR. C. E. COLLINS, L.R.C.P., M.R.C.S., East Grinstead	MR. E. H. MYDDELTON-GAVEY, Tunbridge Wells
SIR JAMES DUKE, Bart., Laughton	MR. F. H. NYE, Broadwater Manor, Worthing
MR. H. S. W. EYRE, St. Leonards-on-Sea	EARL RUSSELL, Chichester
MR. S. FARRER, Hove	MR. A. M. SINGER, Hove
MR. C. F. FROWD, Hastings	MR. W. H. TRIBE, Worthing
Capt. J. G. R. HOMFRAY, Hove	Major R. C. TURNER, Hove
MR. F. GODWIN KING, East Grinstead	MR. G. WILDER, Stansted Park, Emsworth
MR. C. J. LUCAS, Warnham Court, Horsham	

Hon. Treasurer:
MR. B. Y. BEVAN, 6, North Street, Brighton.

Hon. Secretary:
MR. F. MIEVILLE, Summersdale, Chichester.   Telegrams: "Miéville, Chichester."   Telephone: 6, Chichester.

Head-quarters:

Brighton: GRAND HOTEL and OLD SHIP HOTEL	East Grinstead: YE DORSET ARMS HOTEL
Chichester: The DOLPHIN HOTEL	Horsham: The ANCHOR HOTEL
Eastbourne: The GRAND HOTEL	Worthing: WARNE'S HOTEL

Established: January, 1905. Subscription: £2 2s., no entrance fee. Affiliated: A.C.G.B.I. and Motor Union. Annual meeting: January.

MEMBERS (In addition to those above).

Acheson-Gray, Rev. H. A.	Cundy, E. C.	Little, W. G.
Barker, H.	Deck, Dr. E. J.	Lucas, V. R.
Barttelot, Sir W.	Dove, W. H.	McGaw, J.
Baxendale, F. H.	Dugdale, Rev. S.	Mastin, J. F.
Baxendale, G.	Edge, S. F.	Mieville, M. F.
Bearsey, T. A.	Erskine, L.	Miller, J., L.D.S.
Beckwith, R. M.	Evans, J.	Minter, L., M.D.
Biden, A.	Eyre, H. S.	Moore, H.
Boyd, Rev. H. J.	Eyre, R. S. K.	Moore, H. S.
Bradshaw, A. E.	Farrer, S. H.	Newington, Dr. A. S.
Bransom, W.	Foreman, H.	Norman, S. H.
Brassey, Lord	Fox, T. O.	Oakley, Lieut. W. S.
Brown, E. G.	French, M. F.	Osborn, G. W.
Bruton, J. B.	Garrett, T.	Osborn, Sir F., Bart.
Brydges, J. K.	Goodall, A. H.	Osborne, Dr. O.
Buckwell, J. C., J.P.	Goodwin, W. F.	Pape, E. J., F.R.G.S.
Burkhardt, E.	Grace, M. P.	Paravicini, H. F. de
Burnett, R. C.	Greenwood, J. A.	Pearce, W.
Burrows, L. R.	Hall, H. E.	Potts, Rev. F. H.
Caffin, E. E.	Hallows, F. S.	Rucker, M. D.
Campbell, R.	Handley, H.	Russell, T.
Cann, T. P.	Hill, G.	Sadler, F.
Charles, F. E.	Hissey, J. J.	Simmins, G.
Cockerell, J. P.	Johnston, J. P.	Smith, O. B.
Colgate, Lieut.-Colonel H., F.R.C.S.	Jones, S. A.	Snow, Dr. L. M.
	Jowers, R. F.	Soames, E.
Collins, C. E., L.R.C.P., M.R.C.S.	Knight, J.	Solla, J. de
	Lea, W. C.	Spencer, Capt. F. R.
Constable, F.	Leibstein, D. W.	Stockman, G.
Couchman, J. G.	Leith, J. W. B.	Stow, F. S. P.
Cowderoy, W.	Lereculey, J.	Stratton, N.
Cox, W. S., M.D.	Leslie, A.	Sutton, F. B.
Crookshank, E. M., J.P.	Leslie, Major C. M. A.	Swaffer, H. E.

Sussex County Automobile Club—*continued.*

Swaffer, M. T.	Treglown, W. M.	White, F. A.
Taylor, H. H.	Tulk-Hart, Dr. E.	White, J. G.
Teasdale, C. J. T.	Turner, H.	Wilson, C.
Tebb, B. H.	Wallis, W. L.	Wood, C. W.
Townsend, A.	Warne, G. H.	Wright, W. J.
Townsend, S. M.	Webb, E. R.	Yoward, Rev. W. D.

✳ ✳ ✳

The 1906 membership of the Sussex County Automobile Club.

Swift of Coventry specialised in making good-quality light cars. AP 887, registered in August 1905, belonged to Lt-Col. G.E. Maule, of Brunswick Square, Hove, and was the 7/8hp twin-cylinder model.

This large Renault tourer was part of Sir Weetman Pearson's fleet of cars at Paddockhurst. At the wheel is H. Budgen from Turners Hill.

It did not take long for a meritocracy to emerge among the different makes and Napier, aided by racing success, quickly staked a claim to be one of the best British cars. This is a 1905 24hp tourer, whose first owner was E.D. Jordan.

A slightly later Napier is this limousine parked across a deserted Madeira Drive at Brighton. It is not recommended to repeat this pose today. The reverse of the postcard describes it as a 15/20hp, a model not mentioned in reference books. The chain drive dates it prior to 1907: by now Napier had acquired the typical radiator with tall water-filler.

Vulcan was a popular make in East Sussex: this 10hp tonneau was registered in November 1905 to Lady Idena Brassey, of Park Gate, Battle. It is fitted with rear-entrance bodywork, somewhat outmoded by this date.

Mors was a French make which gained prestige through racing successes: this is a 24hp detachable top brougham registered BP 417 to H.F. Bowyer on 15 May 1905.

A pretty little 12hp Star, described as a 'racer', probably more because of its stark coachwork consisting of two bucket seats and bolster fuel tank than for its speed. It is pictured outside the Hovian Engineering Co. Ltd, Denmark Garage, Hove, and was presumably a demonstrator.

Another boy-racer, coincidentally from the same factory, this is a 2-cylinder 10/12hp Briton. As the car looks new, this is presumably Mr C. Smith of Cromwell Road, Hove, who was the first owner in 1909.

Darracq produced a wide range of models and this *c.*1906 tourer shows the trend towards longer chassis, and side entrance bodywork. Registered BP 1161 in West Sussex.

The flavour of Edwardian motoring is well captured by this big Peugeot tourer, photographed at Bishopstone on 16 August 1910. Even the dog is included in the outing, and the boy in front wears the latest line in goggles.

ONE OF OUR FLEET HIRE CARS.

H. PAINE, PHOTO]

GRAND & MARINE GARAGES, OPPOSITE PIER, WORTHING.

[WORTHING.

TELEPHONE NO. 280.

PROPRIETOR, P. G. SIMMONDS.

Until 1908 the pioneer manufacturers Humber built cars in two factories: those emerging from the Beeston plant in Nottinghamshire were the up-market range, compared with the Coventry vehicles. This 20hp Beeston model is distinguishable by its curved bulkhead which extends behind the windscreen. Registered in London, it was available for hire in Worthing.

AP 1849 is a Stuart, a 7hp light car produced between 1906 and 1908 by the Star Cycle Co. of Wolverhampton.

Above: An unidentifiable photograph but included because of its charm: all we know is that the bride's name is Eunice, and her transport to the church is an East Sussex-registered Talbot.

Below: A much smaller example of the Talbot marque is this 8/10hp model of 1907. Its 2-cylinder engine of 1,248cc had to pull quite substantial tourer coachwork. Jackson Bros. of Horsham took delivery of it on 10 July.

Above and below: DY 398 is a 10hp Brennabor 2-seater torpedo of 1912. Its first owner was Dr A.W. Brodribb, of Hastings, whose son is sitting in it. (This little German car survives to this day, and is seen in the second photograph on a post-war Veteran Car Rally somewhere on the Sussex coast.)

Above and below: Two examples of the ubiquitous Model T Ford: above is an early (1909) car, owned by Miss C. Hunter of Brighton, and below a 1910 car with very strange non-standard body, seen at Haywards Heath.

Above and below: Chauffeurs were frequently called on to drive their masters in 2-seater cars: above CD 1324 is a 1911 Lion-Peugeot 16hp, owned by E.R. Hunt of Brighton, and below a Unic of the same period, also Brighton-registered.

Once cars became truly reliable doctors were one of the first professions to use them widely. Here is Dr Alban of Lindfield beside his Renault 8hp AX 2-seater. This was a thoroughly practical and dependable small car, of which many are extant today. The doctor's shoes and the state of the rear mudguard are reminders of the muddy roads, which were commonplace.

Closed cars for the owner-driver were not common till after the First World War: this chic Flanders 15/20 coupé dates from 1912, and belonged to the vicar of Apuldram, near Chichester.

It is always rewarding for the motoring historian to come across rarities when examining old photographs. Even with the naked eye, the words 'STELLA GENEVE' can be made out on the hub. This 1908 landaulette is probably the 10/12hp (3-litre) model and was one of only 200 cars produced by Stella. It lived in Lewes, and its chauffeur, Mr Standing, is at the wheel.

Most Unics were used for hire, and this 12/14hp example of 1910 is no exception, the taximeter being clearly visible. Its owner was P.M.S. Carmichael, of Stratheden Hotel, Regency Square Brighton.

Mr L.H.L.G. Langley of The Holt, Clayton, displayed excellent taste in acquiring this 30hp Turcat-Mery torpedo in 1913. It replaced a 1909 18hp example of the same Marseilles-built marque. The postcard reads, 'Harry has taken this car to Paris'. The white bodywork, a nightmare to clean, is very elegant, and at least ten years ahead of its time. The picture is full of interest – the unusual screen, the huge scuttle-mounted acetylene lamp and early electric headlamps, as well as the elaborate cast-iron brackets supporting the roof of the washdown. Turcat-Méry were involved in racing, and won the first Monte Carlo Rally in 1911.

The controversial S.F. Edge, whose name occurs so often in early UK motoring history, lived at Ditchling. Here he is seen in an elegant example of the Napier, which he so vigorously promoted. It is the 30hp model and dates from 1913.

Around 1912, the 'cyclecar' was born. This 8hp G.W.K. typifies the genre, and, in spite of its unorthodox friction drive, was one of the better and more successful designs. This car belonged to C.J. Kerridge of Hove, and was delivered to him in November 1913. Note the side starting-handle ahead of the rear wheel: the running-board hinges to allow access.

By contrast this 8hp Hopper, also from 1913, is a complete obscurity. Built by F. Hopper & Co. of Barton-on-Humber, it was sold to A.J. Kessler, of Waldegrove Road, Brighton. The make is not recorded in any of the reference books, and therefore it may have been a one-off, albeit very professionally built.

H. Pulham of Sackville Road, St Leonards, had a fleet of hire cars. This 1914 B.S.A. 13.9hp, occupied by two fashionable ladies, is, for its time, very elegant, with the bonnet neatly meeting the swept scuttle. The B.S.A. was a downmarket Daimler, not infrequently used for taxi work. The discreet posies of flowers suggest this one is off to a wedding.

Here is an example of the rather grander Daimler. CD 2138 was registered on 15 July 1913 to Mrs K. Windsor of Brighton, but is almost certainly rather older than that.

Vinot et Deguingand was a French make well liked in this country. This smart tourer with jovial chauffeur belonged to Mrs Julia Meyer of Thakeham. It dates from 1914, and is the 12/14hp model.

Few marques maintained such a consistent tradition for quality as Sunbeam. This 16/20hp, 4-litre example dates from around 1912, and typifies the formal coachwork often carried by these chassis. The licence disc at the foot of the screen tells us that the scene is post 1920, and the car is probably being used for hire.

Left, opposite above and below: Vulcan typified reliable middle-class transport: AP 1689 and AP 3791 successively belonged to the same, now unknown, owner, marque loyalty being common. Opposite below, HC 229, Eastbourne-registered, shows clearly the little blacksmith mascot which was the Vulcan trademark.

Below: BP 3209 is a 1914 Fiat, probably a Tipo Zero.

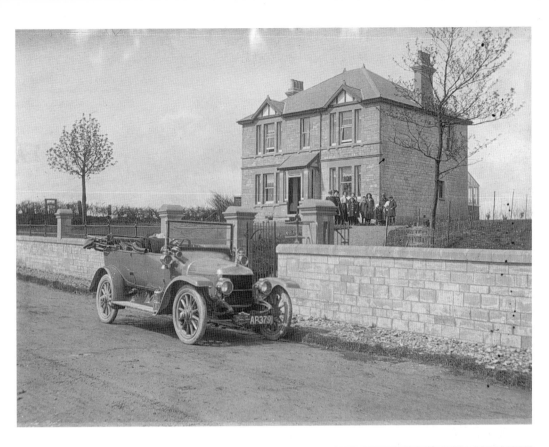

No. 3 Instruction Car, Turberville Motor School   Garage and Works, 53 Dyke Road, Brighton   'Phone 371

Above: The reverse of this postcard reveals that the Turberville Motor School of Dyke Road, Brighton, offered 'private tuition by lady instructors', a welcome innovation no doubt to nervous would–be female motorists. 'No. 3 instruction car' is a French Chenard et Walcker, quite a heavy car for a novice.

Below: AP 4275 is a Darracq of 1914, probably the 20/30hp. Of note is the way that the bonnet slopes upward towards the scuttle (wherein is the petrol tank) to produce more graceful lines. The top panel of the windscreen opens inwards to sit flush with the roof. The young chauffeur poses impassively with rug over his arm.

Above: This 20hp Vauxhall landaulette coachwork of about 1912 carries coachwork by Harris & Others of Clapham and belonged to Mrs Goodhart of Hove.

Below: By 1913, when this fine landaulette first took to the road, Humber were well established as one of the most respected British manufacturers. The car is shown, obviously brand new, outside its unknown coachbuilders, alongside a milk float, a reminder of how the old craftsmen adapted to the new skills of motor body building. Worth noting are the hackney carriage plate below the track rod, and the unusual mudguards, typical of the marque. The length of chassis suggests this is the 28hp model.

Above and below: These two photographs from Brighton provide an insight into aspects of a chauffeur's life less often depicted. Above, two Daimlers, a limousine and a landaulette, are drawn up outside 'Bert Savage's noted house for chauffeurs' – not for the drivers the comfortable hotel accommodation their owners enjoyed. Below a Buick of 1916 stands outside its mews garage, while the chauffeur lovingly polishes it, having first filled it with petrol.

Above and below: From about 1912 American cars were imported in increasing numbers, and the process continued after the war, with British manufacturers hamstrung by shortage of materials and strikes. In the picture above CD 4469 is a 1918 Overland 15hp belonging to Mr A.S. Smith of Brighton, and below is a 1920 Chevrolet '490', owned by Mr T.H. Maltby of Bexhill.

This little 10hp Singer of 1919 has unusual closed coachwork, described as a 'coupé limousine'. It was owned by Edmund Salisbury of Littlehampton.

Best known for much more staid machinery, Hillman of Coventry produced this rakish 10hp speed model, with outside exhaust in 1920. It wasn't all show, either, for Raymond Mays used one to good effect in hillclimbs, and George Bedford had Brooklands successes with a stripped tuned version. This is BP 6577, used in long-distance trials by C.D. Michaelis.

Right: Not a baby Rolls-Royce, despite its aristocratic radiator, but an 11.9hp Albert tourer, pictured at Haywards Heath, CD 7732 was registered to Miss I. Bailey in April 1923, and supplied by Caffyns.

Below: One of the rarer light cars of the 1920s was the Coventry-built Cluley. This 10.5hp example was supplied by J. W. Holloway & Sons of Shoreham in May 1925, and it was photographed when nearly new. An identification feature of Cluleys is the very prominent hubs.

Just why the driver of this Austin 12/4 2-seater is blindfolded we shall never know: presumably he is participating in a motor gymkhana and being guided verbally by his passenger on the running board. Mr W. Marchant of Lindfield was the photographer.

Many early garages sprang up behind inns, and this photograph of a pair of Ford Model Ts at the Lamb Garage, Rustington, makes the point. Each carries a hackney carriage plate above the front axle, while the garage logo is a swastika. This card illustrates a pitfall for historians: the left-hand car has a registration dating from 1906, which has been transferred to this c.1919 vehicle, whereas the other car has a 1920 issue plate, appropriate for its age.

Above and below: The brilliant little Austin 7 provided an introduction to motoring for so many, the author included. Above is a 1926 chummy, below a 1930 tourer. The latter sports a horn ring, a bird mascot on the radiator core, and RAC and AA badges as accessories.

One of the classiest of the new breed of small cars which emerged in the early 1920s was the Humber 8/18. This Brighton-registered 2-seater dates from 1925.

Anything but classy was the Trojan, an ugly, noisy, slow and unorthodox device which had the priceless virtues of dependability and great torque at low speeds. This example was delivered by the Lewes Motor Works to Mr Selmes, proprietor of the Crossing Inn, Mountfield.

The Hotchkiss, despite its name, was a French-made quality car. PM 7912 is a 1927 AM 2 coupé belonging to W.B. Marshall of Scaynes Hill.

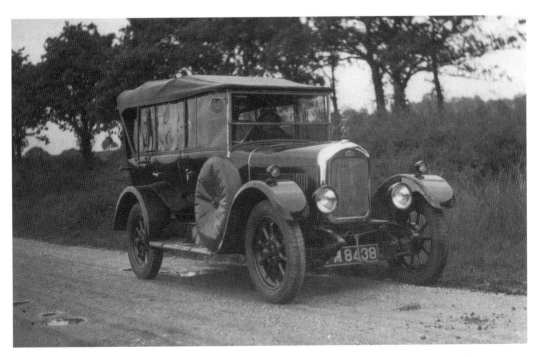

The sum of £220 was required to buy this Singer 10/26 when new in 1927. A step up from the Austin 7, in size if perhaps not in quality, it was a popular model. Note the AA badge on the filler cap, the spare wheel cover, and the snug weather equipment. The first owner was E.G. Smith of Hove.

Above and below: One of the most popular American imports between the wars was the Buick. Above is a standard 20/58 of 1926 (new to T.S. Inglis of Felbridge Hotel, East Grinstead); below is a 1925 27.3hp with English all-weather coachwork painted dark green. Its aristocratic owner was Lady Catherine Ashburnham, the last of the family to own Ashburnham Place, near Battle, and the car is posed in the stable yard beside the ancestral coach, with the church tower just visible behind.

Above and below: The Italian firm of O.M. produced successful side-valve sports cars during the 1920s. This example, dating from May 1927, was the less common 4-cylinder 10/30 model, and belonged to an enthusiast called John Pole. Below is another desirable Italian car he owned, a 1926 Alfa Romeo 22/90 sports.

Above and below: A pair of photographs which demonstrate the roominess of cars in the 1920s. The Jowett (above) registered UF 3855 is only 907cc, but has more room than modern luxury cars; whilst the Bullnose Morris Oxford, seen at Goodwood Racecourse in 1927, has enough room in the back to carry luggage as well as passengers (as was often done).

Whereas the Jowett shown on the previous page was a really worthy light car, the Clyno 9 (seen above in tourer form) was, from all accounts, cheap and nasty, its fabric body being of particularly poor quality. This car is being raffled for one shilling, and no doubt some cynics suggested that was more than its value. In fact, Clyno had produced very acceptable vehicles in very large numbers during the mid-1920s, but this Century model (sold for £112 10s 0d) was their swansong. Closer inspection of the picture reveals that the photograph was taken outside Queen's Hotel, Hastings; that the car was donated by the employees of Timpson's, the coach company; and that the raffle was in aid of the Royal East Sussex and Buchanan Hospital.

By contrast with the Clyno, this Riley Monaco, also of 9hp RAC rating, was an outstanding car. As the owner of an identical car, the author may be biased, but its performance, brakes and handling were (and are) remarkable. PN 4231 was registered new to A. Mitchell of Forest Row, in August 1929.

ASHDENE GARAGE,
HURST GREEN

Cars for Hire 4d. per mile,
(Minimum 2/6).

Above: At the end of the 1920s, there was a brief but significant vogue for fabric bodies. This 1928 Hillman 14 illustrates the genre well. It is parked outside Ashdene Garage, Hurst Green, whence it could be hired. The owner's bungalow doubles up as the office.

Below: Harringtons, of 89 Church Street, Brighton, and who later moved to Hove, built the striking dual green sports saloon shown here. The chassis was a Beverley 22/90 (the make formerly known as Beverley-Barnes). With an 8-cylinder 3-litre engine, this car was shown at the 1929 and 1930 Motor Shows, and then sold to Sir Peter Hoare, Bart. The design exhibits typical features of the period: shallow windscreen, the newly popular inbuilt boot and an intricate two-colour paint scheme. Harringtons were founded in 1897, and were best known for their bus and coach bodies. They closed in 1966.

Above: Of 1931 vintage (but pictured during the Second World War with its headlamp deflector fitted) is this 20hp Daimler PN 7853, bought new by R.K. Henderson of Seaford.

Below: Photographed at Rottingdean (by J.J. Hill of Newhaven) is an Eastbourne-registered Rover 10. At this period (*c.*1933) Rover had yet to gain its reputation for middle-class quality.

A delightful picnic scene sets off this Morris Cowley coupé, a 1932 model. The photograph was taken between Eastbourne and Lewes on 28 April 1933.

This Ford 10 is parked on the A285 at Upwaltham in August 1935, where it would be foolhardy to stop today!

This lady with her furs is fully conscious that her Triumph Gloria is the right sort of car to pose with to attract attention. NJ 3159 was first registered in March 1934 to the Hon. J.S. Colville, of Danegate House, Eridge.

A powerful and impressive car, this Vauxhall 20 was delivered in March 1935 to F.W. Serres of Hove.

The Cut Mill Garage, Ltd.

BOSHAM, SUSSEX.

Reg. Office:—CUT MILL.   Telephone Bosham 120.

Main Agents for Fiat.

Agents for Austin, Ford, Hillman, Vauxhall.

£3

Directors:—

A. HAWLEY SAVAGE, A.M.I.E.T.
J. C. L. VERLEY, M.I.C.E.
W. H. C. WATSON.

14th April 1937

B. Durling Esq.,
The Swan Hotel,
Bosham.

To 1937 Popular Ford 8 h.p. colour Black as per Manufacturers specification	100..0..0
Petrol & Oil put in car at factory by Messrs Ford Co.Ltd.,	10..0
Number Plates	1..0..0
Licence Holder	3..0
	101.13..0
Less allowance on Riley	85..0..0
	£16.13..0

13. April. 1937
BOSHAM, SUSSEX. 547
From B. Durling Esq
the sum of Sixteen pounds
thirteen shillings pence
For Cut Mill Garage, Ltd.
£ 16: 13:0

For a short period in the mid-1930s one could buy a Ford 8 for the magic figure of £100. Just why Mr Durling, of the Swan Hotel, Bosham, preferred one to his Riley we shall never know.

Of only 569cc, the little Fiat 500 cabriolet, nicknamed 'La Topolino' (Mickey Mouse) was of advanced design, with hydraulic brakes and independent front suspension. It sold for £120 in the UK. Its diminutive size is emphasised by the height of the lady driver of this 1938 West Sussex-registered example.

The Buick marque continued to have a strong following in the UK up till the Second World War. Shown is a 1939 8-cylinder Sedan, registered to Mr J.L. Reid, of Stonegate near Ticehurst.

By 1939, British small cars had become rather dull, with none of the innovation shown by Continental manufacturers. This Austin 8, successor to the 7 and Big 7, is typical of the breed.

By turning a blind eye to our self-imposed cut-off date of the Second World War, we can include this picture of a Sussex-built car. The B.M.A. Hazelcar, built by Gates & Pearson of Alice Street, Hove, was a short-lived attempt in the early 1950s to produce an electric-powered car. Only six were made (it was expensive at £535, slow – no more than 20mph – and had a limited range of 50-60 miles before needing a recharge). This one was optimistically entered in the RAC 1,000 miles rally, a far cry from the thinly disguised racing machines which enter today.

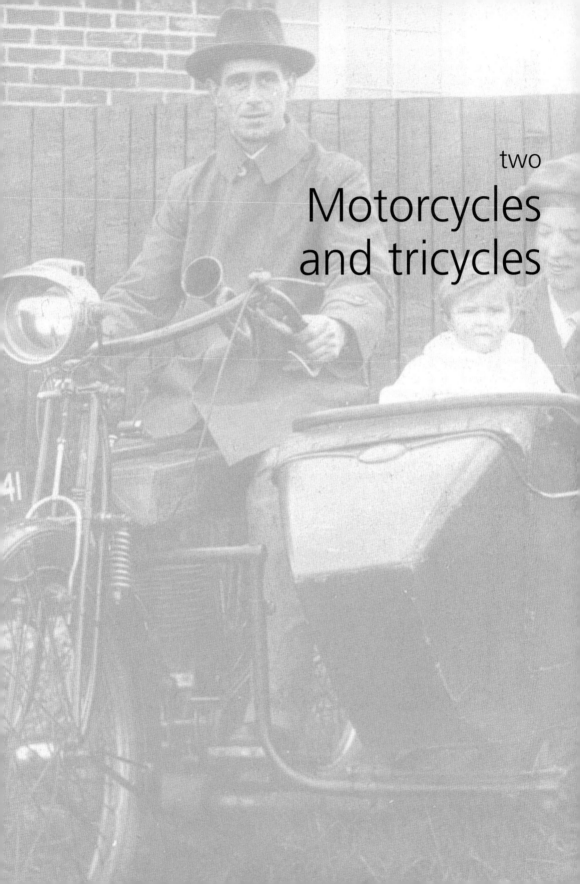

two

Motorcycles and tricycles

It was not uncommon in the early years of the twentieth century for enthusiastic amateurs to build their own motorcycles, which appear in the registration records as 'own make'. Frank Rubie Stocks of Rye was one such character and this single-cylinder machine, dating from 1908, was his second attempt.

Rex (Latin for king, of course) was one of the pioneer British motorcycle manufacturers. This is a 5hp v-twin example, dating from 1906.

The identity of this tricycle is not known, for the West Sussex records only record the machine to which BP 924 was later transferred. This does not detract from the photograph as a splendid period piece.

In the early years of the twentieth century there was a huge number of ephemeral makes of motorcycle which sprang up: typically a bicycle agent might start assembling a few machines from bought-in components. Shaw & Son of High Street, Crawley, was a Sussex firm that made a brave attempt at motorcycle production, and during the gestation period of this book an excellent photograph of one of their tricars came into the author's hands. The crankcase of the single-cylinder engine bears the name 'Shaw & Son', showing that this was no mere assembly of other people's components. The photograph is full of interest, not least the radiator mounted behind the saddle which cools the cylinder head, and the basketwork seat for the brave passenger. There is one other tantalising question raised by this picture. The original was displayed on a large framed montage of early motoring photographs which hung above the desk of William Morris, later Lord Nuffield, at his Oxford garage in Longwall Street. Did this Shaw forecar by any chance belong to the great man?

Above: The forecar, a 3-wheeler on motorcycle lines with the passenger seated ahead of the driver, was briefly popular around 1903 to 1906 but turned out to be a blind alley. Whereas the Shaw made no attempt to hide its motorcycle ancestry, this Rexette sports stylish flared wings, and a swept-out cowling around the rear wheel and engine. Wheel steering rather than handlebars is employed. Mr A.E. Marriott of Hastings purchased this example in May 1905, having transferred the DY 15 registration number from an earlier Rex forecar.

Above: A lovely study of a 1914 Royal Ruby 2½hp, whose attractive rider is nineteen-year-old Miss Beatrice Quick, daughter of Alfred Quick who had the first car in Horsham. She is believed to have been the first lady in England to be featured in a motorcycle manufacturer's catalogue, being shown on this very machine by the Royal Ruby company.

Opposite below: The James motorcycle, made in Birmingham, was produced between 1902 and 1964, an unusually long run: Mr L.C. Traylen of Battle bought this 4¼hp combination on 1 January 1916. The trilby would seem to be somewhat unsuitable headgear.

Royal Enfield earned a good reputation as makers of high-quality machines. This 2¾hp machine predates the First World War by a couple of years or so, though it was registered in 1920.

Two Signals officers are seen aboard a *c*.1914 Zenith Gradua 3½hp. This was famous for its variable gearing, whereby an engine pulley with adjustable effective diameter was worked by the 'coffee-grinder' handle above the fuel tank, with simultaneous correction of the length of the driving belt made by sliding the rear wheel backwards or forwards in the rear fork slots.

Premier of Coventry was a significant name before the First World War in British motorcycling, building their own engines as on this 1913 example. There is much of interest in the detail: the riders practical apparel, including leggings, the stylish wickerwork sidecar, with acetylene light on the prow, the mirror (quite unusual), AA badge and Union flag.

Almost obliterating a 1920 Douglas machine are a bevy of beauties photographed at Worthing in 1923. The flimsy light coloured clothing looks singularly inappropriate for motorcycling – perhaps they were just posing.

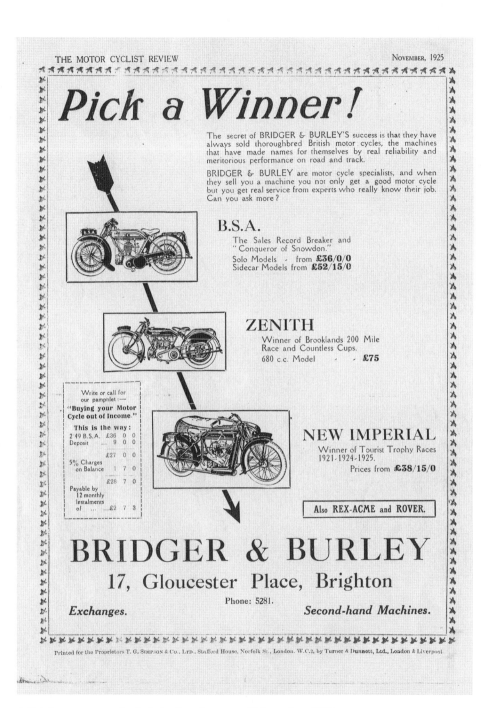

A Brighton motorcycle dealer's advertisement of November 1925.

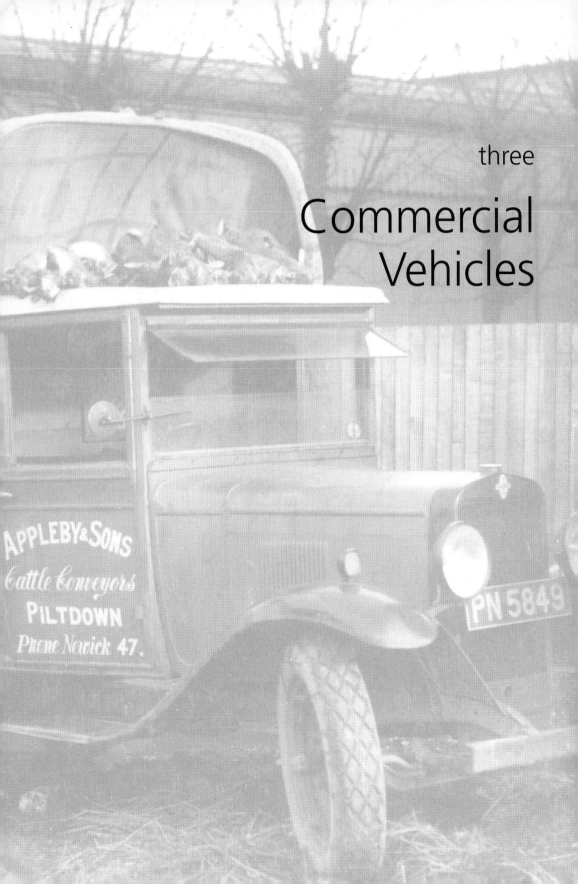

three

Commercial
Vehicles

This splendid, solid-tyred Ensign lorry of around 1915 was owned by the Stoner family of Hurstpierpoint, and is shown in the yard behind the former Lamb public house in that village.

This is an unusual view of Brighton Fire Brigade's motor tender, new in October 1909, and designed by themselves. From the registration records, we find it was built on a Star 30/40hp chassis. There is almost nothing for the crew to cling to as it sped to an emergency.

The Hove Brigade had a Merryweather fire-engine, here seen in action. The combination of enormous weight, narrow solid tyres with no tread, and road surfaces like that in the picture, must have made it potentially lethal.

Far and away the most popular light van of the early 1920s was the Model T Ford. Here is a smart example owned by a Brighton business. Mead & Co's van is on the longer one-ton chassis, and was used for furniture removals (preferably not grand pianos).

In addition to their utility cars, Trojan produced light vans, in which the leisurely pace of which the design was capable was less of a disadvantage. This example has been smartly sign-written, and belonged to a Horsham grocer and pork purveyor who specialised in alliteration using the letter P.

The Dennis was a comparatively local make, built at Guildford. Lintott & Son of Horsham owned this sturdy 1926 example. Running on solid tyres it had an engine of 6,235cc, and a worm-driven back-axle. The chassis price was £750.

Also on a Dennis chassis is this interesting example of an early breakdown truck, belonging to Mansfield's of Eastbourne. It dates from the late 1920s: prior to this most recovery vehicles were conversions of large-engined cars.

The following four pictures all show commercial vehicles supplied by Mansfield's of Eastbourne. Above is a Chevrolet 10cwt van of 1928, looking dated on its wooden wheels, owned by Belgravia Dairy of Latimer Road, Eastbourne: the coach-painting, showing a cow and milk bottle, is typical of the period.

Just £120 bought this 5cwt Singer Junior van, supplied new to a Polegate bakery. Singer only ever dabbled in commercials, and this is quite an unusual vehicle. Note the phone number Polegate 7: today it would be necessary to remember 11 digits to reach such a business.

Above and below: Two contrasting Chevrolet lorries: above is a 1930 LQ 30cwt example belonging to Appleby & Sons of Piltdown, cattle conveyors. On the roof is an array of dead rabbits. Below is a 6-wheeled furniture van, of strangely ugly proportions, owned by an Eastbourne removals firm.

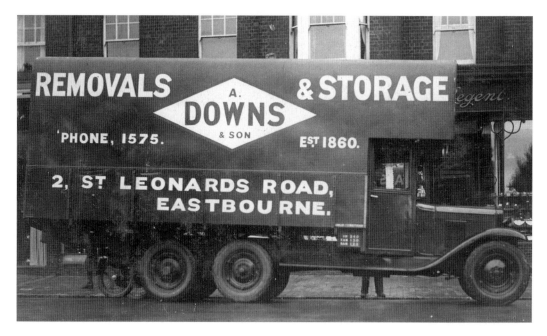

Above and below: Really small vans began with the Austin 7, and the Morris 5 cwt, on the Minor chassis, came on the scene in 1929. Shown here are examples of each, both owned by wireless stores. The Austin is above, and the Morris, of Brighton Radio Stores, 2 Hampton Street, below.

The Ford Model A was the successor to the legendary Model T. Whereas the private car version never achieved the popularity of its forerunner, the commercials were a familiar sight on British roads. This example, nicely posed in a working environment, dates from 1929, and belonged to N. Rowland & Sons of Horsham, described as 'Wood, Hoop and Broom Merchants'.

Rather half-heartedly dressed up for the 1938 Littlehampton Carnival is this two-year-old AEC Monarch Mark II lorry of South Coast Carriers.

four

Buses and
Coaches

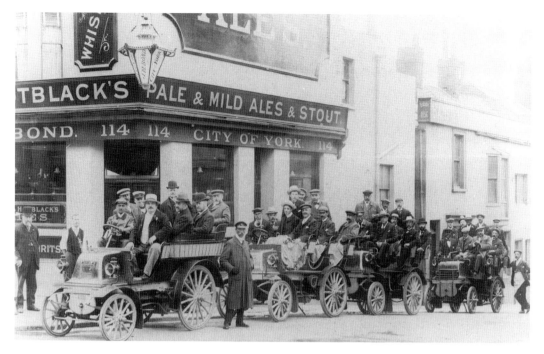

The City of York public house in Western Road, Brighton, provides the backdrop for this *c*.1900 photograph of M.M.C. or Daimler wagonettes (the makes are almost identical). Number plates had not yet been introduced, and the vehicles feature chain drive, solid tyres, and large rear wheels. Sprags, which were lowered under the chassis to prevent running back out of control on hills, are visible on two vehicles. The angled steering columns on the first two are a modification: by contrast the rear bus has tiller steering. All the passengers are male, and all sport some form of headgear.

Three Milnes-Daimler charabancs with the tiered seating favoured at the time provide transport for the Cootham Sunday School Outing on 11 August 1910. The Milnes-Daimler, a joint venture between the German Daimler company, and the British firm G.F. Milnes & Co. was a reliable and popular early bus chassis.

Worthing Motor Services was the forerunner of Southdown. This 20-seater Milnes–Daimler coach, CD 338, was new in 1905, and ran between Worthing and Brighton. Note that there is a glass partition across the vehicle halfway along the chassis, and a W.M.S. pennant on the roof above the driver.

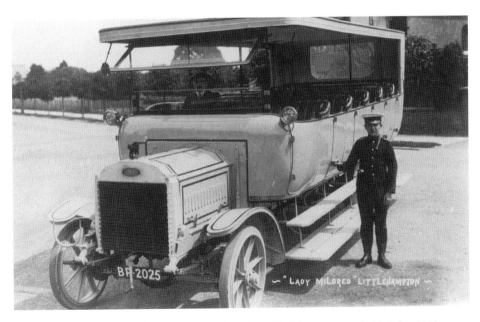

Charles Norris pioneered charabanc excursions from Littlehampton, and this is his 1912 Dennis, named 'Lady Mildred'. Unusually, it has a detachable roof rather than a cumbersome hood; its smart lines are marred somewhat by the massive protruding running boards, which extend well outside the wheels.

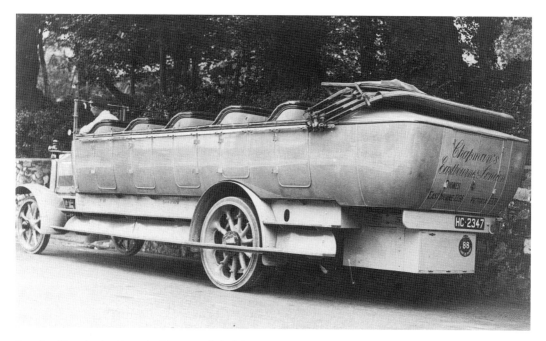

Another Dennis charabanc is this example belonging to Chapman's of Eastbourne, HC 2347. Chapman's pioneered long-distance coach tours, including trips to the Continent, and this vehicle has the unusual feature of a luggage compartment at the rear. The company was taken over by Southdown in 1930.

The Ford Model T in standard form could only accommodate the smallest of charabanc bodies. Here such a vehicle, the forerunner of the minibus, carries a troupe of pierrots in Hastings in 1913.

Here is one for those who enjoy solving a mystery. The identity of the manufacturer of this ungainly charabanc has defeated the bus experts: the Eastbourne registration records are not available, and the only clue is the LGOC B-type radiator. Answers on a postcard…..

A Straker-Squire COT/5 of 1915 with Beadle coachwork, and belonging to Southdown stands at Cuckfield, awaiting the journey back to Brighton. Note the luggage rack on the roof.

Registered BP 5871 is this small American Garford charabanc of A.F. Lewis of Chichester, dating from 1920.

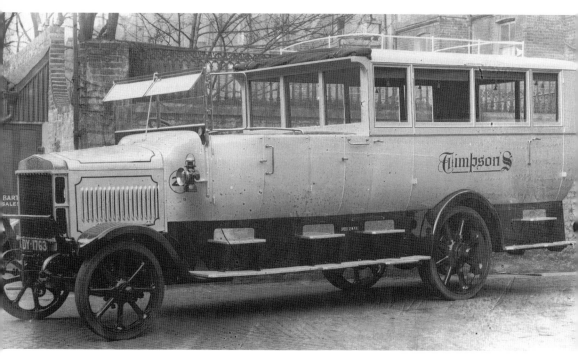

DY1763 is a 1921 Karrier with most unusual bodywork by James Bartle. It looks as if the coachbuilders had second thoughts after the second row of charabanc seats, and decided to enclose the rest. Timpson's were a well-known operator of coaches between London and Hastings. The Karrier is finished in their silver livery.

Bus and charabanc bodies were mounted on all manner of improbable chassis. This smart vehicle is an Itala, an Italian marque more famous for its racing cars. It was owned by Rowland of Worthing, and ran for just one year, 1921.

Southdown's Tilling-Stevens TS3 CD 4861 took to the road in March 1919, and carries a body acquired from London General. The TS3 was one of the famous petrol-electric buses, and this one is seen at the Worthing garage. Pratt's pretroleum was later rebranded as Esso.

Photographed at Southdown's Eastbourne garage is a Leyland Model N, which started life in 1919, but was rebodied by Harrington's of Hove in 1923. The saloon top is detachable. The notice at the rear boasts that the coach has 'armchair seats, electric light, and pneumatic tyres.'

In the 1920s, hundreds of small country operators sprang up – and usually disappeared just as quickly! This is the very varied fleet of E.E. Piper, of Dicker Garage Hellingly. From right to left, the vehicles are 1927 Graham Dodge 20-seater, 1927 Dennis 20-seater, 1927 Overland 14-seater, and at the back, a Chevrolet.

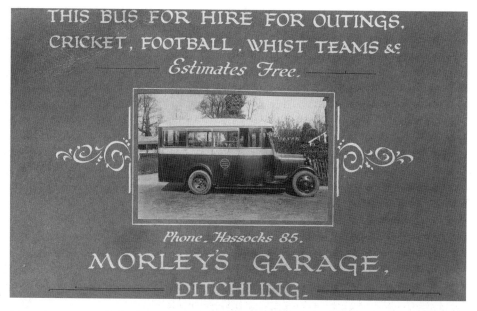

THIS BUS FOR HIRE FOR OUTINGS,
CRICKET, FOOTBALL, WHIST TEAMS &c
Estimates Free.

Phone. Hassocks 85.
MORLEY'S GARAGE,
DITCHLING.

It was not uncommon in the 1920s for a village to have its own resident bus, which might alternate between trips to the nearest towns on market day, and private hire use. Morley's garage at Ditchling were sufficiently proud of their Ford Model A to produce this advertising postcard. Its regular run was to Hassocks Station.

This odd little vehicle, looking rather like a bus shelter on castors, is in fact a Guy, built in
Wolverhampton. There was a vogue in the mid-1920s, pioneered by Shelvoke & Drewry, for small
buses of this type, which usually operated along sea-fronts. The Guy, owned by the famous Magnus
Volk, is seen at the Devil's Dyke, and dates from 1925.

Photographed when new at the coachbuilders, having just received its Brush body, is this 1929
Leyland Titan TD1 of the Southdown fleet. Instead of the multi-national advertising often seen
today, there were boards promoting local stores.

Only an upmarket hotel like the Grand at Eastbourne would have run a smart private bus like this Commer Centaur. It would have been an indication of some social standing to have had this particular bus meet you at the station.

Excursion work was important for Southdown who served a popular holiday area. This fine shot of a Leyland Tiger TS7 on a trip to Dicker Pottery captures well the elegant lines of this 1936-built coach.

five

Street Scenes

A flock of sheep is unlikely to be encountered in Lewes High Street today, but to Mr Every, in his 1905 Decauville 12/14hp tonneau, it was not an unexpected hazard.

As a horse-drawn landau makes its way over the half-open level crossing at Wilmington, the photographer's car, a 14hp Climax tourer, is parked by the roadside. The Climax was an ephemeral Coventry make which lasted but two years.

This wonderfully evocative picture of the Brambletye Hotel garage dates from 1911/1912. The big Talbot tourer towers over two early examples of the 'cyclecar': a Bedelia tandem 2-seater, belt driven, and steered from the rear seat, and an Autotrix 8hp 3-wheeler, a marque of which some thirty examples were built in Weybridge.

A pair of 15hp Darracq tourers make their way off the ferry across the Arun at Littlehampton (replaced by a bridge in 1909). BP 447 belonged to Mr P. Clayton, of Littlehampton, and BP 585 to E. W. Briggs of Worthing.

Not the best photograph technically in this collection, this shot of an early chain-driven tonneau-bodied veteran car is included for the atmosphere of pioneer motoring it conjures up. This gradient on the minor road which approaches Warninglid from the south would go unnoticed today, but represented 'a stiff climb' for a veteran car with three up. The Rifleman public house is no longer there.

A chauffeur sits patiently in the sun outside the Kings Head at Chailey in a Beeston Humber tourer of around 1907, whilst the owner of a 12hp Wolseley waits for his man to make some adjustments.

Waiting at the end of the tramway at Cooden is a 1908 Vinot et Deguingand 16hp tulip phaeton. Registered DY 225, it belonged to R.J. Chandler of Crowhurst.

Daimler and A.C. head a line of cars outside The George, a coaching inn on the old Brighton Road in Crawley. Further along is Shaw's Motor Works.

A Belsize taxi waits beside the Rendezvous Café at Peacehaven, perhaps to convey a prospective purchaser to one of the newly marked out building plots.

This postcard is of the vehicle park at Wannock Gardens near Polegate and boasts that forty charabancs can be accommodated. Foremost is a Napier, followed by Studebaker and Model T Ford. The picture dates from around 1922.

Drawn up in High Hurstwood, outside the Post Office cum general stores cum garage, are a pair of the ubiquitous Model T Fords. DY 2987 is a tourer (perhaps the car advertised for hire) and PM 4343 is a van, bearing an OXO advert on the side.

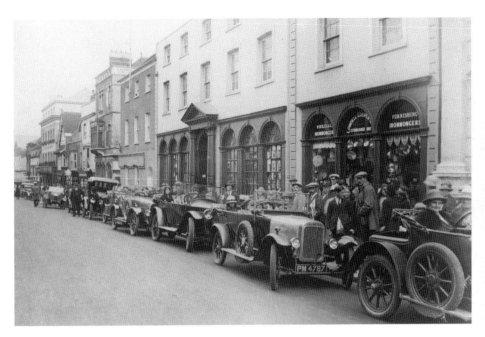

The cars shown here in 1924 in Lewes High Street are about to set off on the 'Cripples'
Outing', perhaps to the nearby coast. PM 4787 is the 1924 10.8hp Clyno of Mr P.E Muller
of Chiddingly, finished in navy blue with polished aluminium bonnet. Behind are Essex, Fiat,
Ford Model T and Morris.

Photographed in 1927 is this line-up of vehicles promoting 'Shopping Week' in Lewes High
Street. A Ford Model T mail van leads a Fiat 501 towing a caravan.

An Aveling & Porter Steam roller (CD 6179) dominates this scene of the construction of the A259 below Roedean School. Note the railway track on the left, constructed to bring materials to the site.

THE MAIN ROAD, CAMBER - ON - SEA.

There is much to catch the eye in this late 1920s picture of Camber: the petrol pump, the casual parking, the surprising number of cars. In the foreground are a pair of Singers, a Junior and a c.1920 10hp 2-seater and two Austin 7s are also visible.

Until well after the Second World War, Bury Hill was a formidable obstacle to the slower car or more nervous driver. Long, steep and narrow, queues quickly built up on summer weekends. Here a Sunbeam pulls out to overtake a 7.5hp Citröen after the top bend.

Plenty here for the ardent car-spotter as the photographer captures the atmosphere of a summer's day market at The Crown, Heathfield. In the foreground, left to right, are Austin 7, Standard 9, Morris Cowley, Ford T, Humber and Austin.

This shot of Bognor, surely taken on a Bank Holiday, is included to show the extraordinary line-up of coaches and charabancs, and the crowds they disgorged. Austin 12, Rover and Essex cautiously make their way through the holidaymakers.

This Singer 12/6 seen at Sharpthorne near West Hoathly was registered to J. Hamilton, of Queens Road, Brighton, in October 1932. Apparently a photographer's car, it appears in a number of Sussex street scenes on postcards.

A Trojan van is parked outside Dean's Stores and Post Office at County Oak, north of Crawley on the Sussex/Surrey boundary.

Standard, Austin 7 Swallow and Clyno feature in The Ship car park at Itchenor.

The lovely High Street in Burwash, forever linked with Kipling, whose home was Batemans, close to the village, is deserted but for a motorcycle and an Austin Light 12/4 Harley saloon. What a contrast with today, when a car park has had to be provided.

Immediately recognisable to those who know the area, this fountain at Fulking carries an appropriate verse from Psalm 105, and is unchanged today. The car is a Morris Minor.

six

Motoring and
Social Events

Left: One can assert confidently that the first motoring event to take place on Sussex soil was the famous Emancipation Run of 1896, forerunner of the Veteran Car Runs from London to Brighton that commemorate it each November. Photographs of the vehicles in transit across Sussex are almost non-existent: shown here is a finisher's medal from that original run.

Brighton Motor Trials,   July. 1905.

Brighton Motor Trials,   July, 1905.

Above, below and opposite below: These fine pictures show competitors at the start of the July 1905 Trials. Opposite below (left to right) Darracq 15, Leon Bollée, Beaufort and Rover 8. Above (left to right) Daimler 30 (Mrs Lloyd) and Orleans 24 (Capt. Skeffington-Smith). Below (left to right) Delahaye 25, James & Browne 18 (T.B. Browne) and Cadillac 8½ (F.S. Bennett). It was normal to carry passengers at such events.

Above and below: Predating the Brighton event by one year were the Speed Trials held at Bexhill. Above we see spectators at the inaugural 1902 event (the car on the left is an early Peugeot and on the right a Decauville). Below is a general view of the start of the 1907 event, of which *The Autocar* wrote, 'We cannot characterise it as likely to advance or popularise motor racing... the extremely lax manner in which the meeting was handled, the utter lack of punctuality, and the dreary waits drove the majority of the audience away long before the end.'

Above and below: On 20 March, 1909, the A.A. organised the transport of a contingent of the Brigade of Guards from London to Hastings by car, to prove the effectiveness of motor transport. The upper picture shows the snowy conditions, and a very spartan looking Deasy: the lower the column nearing its destination.

Above: The first re-enactment of the Emancipation Run to Brighton took place in November 1927, sponsored by the *Daily Sketch* and *Sunday Graphic.* Some of the forty-four cars which started no longer survive, like this heavily modified 1902 De Dion Bouton of V. Ballardine, seen approaching Brighton near the pylons.

Opposite above: Speed hillclimb events, officially sanctioned by the RAC, the governing body for motor sport, were held on public roads as late as 1925. West Sussex hosted one of the most famous of these hillclimbs, at South Harting, starting on the southern edge of the village, and following the route of what is now the B2141 where the road forks. The average gradient was 1 in 12, the steepest 1 in 6.7, and eleven events were held at the venue, the earliest in 1904, and the last in 1924.

This picture is of the 1914 event: few would recognise the location because the road now runs through woodland. The casual disposition of the parked cars and motorcycles, and especially of the spectators- despite there being a competitor (a Morris-Oxford) climbing the hill- is noteworthy. Light cars predominate in the foreground, two Singers and a Swift being discernible.

Opposite below: Some wonderfully evocative pictures have been provided by Edward Reeves, photographers of Lewes, of another, less well known, speed hill-climb. Held at Kidd's Hill (also known as Pipingford Hill) on the road which runs up on to Ashdown Forest from Coleman's Hatch, over a distance of 1,320 yards, the event was organised by the Kent & Sussex Light Car Club on 5 August 1922. This hill, with a maximum gradient of 1 in 6, was first used in 1906. No excuse is needed for including a number of pictures of what was a very minor event, both because of their rarity and because they show so well the relaxed nature of these hill-climbs, with no spectator protection and the pedestrian nature of some of the competing cars, like Mr Deverall's Albert 11.9hp. His time was 2 minutes 44.8 seconds, an average speed of only 16mph – no wonder the car is in focus! The full complement of passengers would not have helped.

Another car with no sporting pretensions is the oil-cooled v-twin 9hp Belsize-Bradshaw of Mr Gibbins. Note the two lads on the right within a couple of feet of the cars, and the unmade road surface.

Somewhat quicker would have been this 1922 Amilcar, an early example of a distinguished small French sporting car.

This shot of competitors (and a non-competing Wolseley 7hp twin-cylinder, wearing trade plates) is full of interest. The aluminium-bodied sports cars are both G.N.s. No.12, named 'Ichthus' (Greek for fish) was driven by Humphries, and behind it is G.L. Hawkins' car, named 'Silver Gnat', which made best time of the day.

Looking in the opposite direction, with the course rising in the background, are a Belsize-Bradshaw and an ABC. Note the policeman, whose co-operation was essential.

A final shot of the Kidd's Hill event shows a stripped 1920 GN driven by E. W. Foster; these air-cooled v-twin cyclecars were surprisingly fast, and popular for use in speed trials, and Foster took second place in his class.

Race Hill, on the South Downs west of Lewes, was a popular venue for speed trials, used from 1925 to 1939, with three or four meetings annually. This view shows the town, with the castle in the background. The start banner may be seen in the centre above the cars.

At the start of the Lewes Speed Trial held on 21 October 1933 is a real thoroughbred: one of the 1½ litre 8-cylinder Delage G.P. cars, driven by Capt. J.C. Davis. The car was 'not quite behaving', and his time was fourth fastest.

Clive Windsor-Richards was a regular pre-war competitor in his Vauxhall 30/98 OE 184. Registered PM 8115 to H.E. Marsh of Bexhill in May 1925, it was rebodied as shown by Owens of Chiswick (and survives to this day in the USA). Here it is competing at Lewes in 1939.

Above and below: The RAC rallies of the 1930s were quite gentle affairs and therefore attracted some ponderous and unlikely cars as competitors. Above, a lumbering Austin 18, driven by C.F. Dingwall, undertakes a reversing test on the front at Eastbourne, at the conclusion of the 1935 event. Two years earlier, Mrs M. Riley takes her more nimble Riley Monaco through the Stop and Restart test at Hastings (below).

Above: Disguised as a bird for the 1905 Bexhill Floral Parade is Earl de la Warr's 18hp Daimler.

Below: This evocative Edwardian scene shows the marriage of Miss Turner, from Sheffield Park Timber Yard, at Nutley church. Waiting to bear the happy couple away is a Deasy landaulette, followed by a Renault.

Above and below: These poignant pictures (one taken as early as 1 September 1914) show wounded soldiers being delivered to a makeshift hospital at the Grammar School in Dyke Road, Brighton. Unic, Fiat and Daimler line up in the upper picture, and below, ironically, a German Benz ambulance unloads.

Above and below: Two elaborate entries for the 1923 Brighton carnival are (above) a lorry elaborately decorated to promote Duresco 'The Top Dog of Water Paints' and (below) an Overland Four pulling a float, the particular significance of which is now obscure.

When the village of Patcham was incorporated into the County Borough of Brighton, the well-known pylons were erected to mark the northern boundary of the town on the A23. The Duke of York, later George VI, who 'opened' them, rides not in a Daimler, but in a Manchester-built Crossley 20.9 Canberra landaulette. A second Crossley follows. The date is 1 April 1928.

seven

Mishaps

The Edwardians did not consider it bad form to turn accidents to good account as postcard subjects. In this case we are fortunate that 'Alice', who sent it, saw fit to note both the details of the mishap and the registration no. of the car. It was a 1903 12hp Daimler tonneau, whose chain drive to the rear axle is clearly visible. It was owned by Kenneth Matlin, Eastbourne. 'Don't often see a motor in this plight, front wheels were broken and axle too; it entered next garden to ours, turned round and backed into ours, then turned over.' The card was posted on 12 December 1904 from East Grinstead, and the accident is unlikely to have happened much earlier than that.

This photograph shows the sad remains of a 24hp Napier, after it fell over the cliff at Galley Hill, Bexhill. The faces of the onlookers in this photograph by Emil Vidler reward closer scrutiny: whilst enjoying the excitement, they manage to retain a degree of gravity.

In 1906, a Milnes-Daimler double-deck bus crashed on Handcross Hill: ten lives were lost, and twenty-two were badly injured. That tragedy has been so well documented that it was decided to depict here a comparatively minor accident instead. Also in 1906, on 20 January, this Milnes Daimler of the Sussex Motor Road Car Co. made a neat job of demolishing a wall at Storrington.

A Foden steam lorry has run out of control in 1915 at the Bottleneck in Lewes High Street with disastrous results.

A Chenard et Walcker laundaulette is seen in an undignified pose in Station Street, Lewes, in 1913. At first sight damage seems slight, but a rear spring is detached, a wheel broken, and the hood partly collapsed and torn.

It is unclear why this 12/14hp Unic taxi from Brighton has charged the hedge: its journey is clearly at an end.

This spectacular accident took place on the A29 north of Slinfold. The turning to Rowhook is behind the camera. An A.C. light car and a Beardmore taxi are locked together – presumably the latter attempted to cross the main road and was struck by the A.C. Note the teacup on the running-board.

Caffyn's breakdown truck, a Vulcan, has been called to recover an over-turned Morris Cowley 2-seater (HC 4905). The usual crowd of onlookers has gathered, at the junction of Enys Road and St Anne's Road, Eastbourne. The date is 1925.

The Austin 7 van seen ignominiously on its side outside Tate Bros garage at Portslade was supplied new to J.&H. Robinson of Hove in 1938. The distinctive features of the chassis are clearly shown.

Buses with their higher ground clearance could often negotiate floods which would defeat lesser vehicles. Here a Straker-Squire of the Brighton Hove & Preston Omnibus Co. encounters a flood at Shoreham, on its route from Worthing to Brighton. The date is 6 November 1911.

Floods have been a recurring problem since long before global warming, and here a Ford Model T truck owned by Lulham & Sons of Brighton gingerly negotiates the flooded Adur at Bramber. The horse and trap behind is clearly better equipped to cope!

Amusement for everyone except the unfortunate driver of this Ford 10, who like many before and since has failed to heed the high tide warnings at Bosham.

BLERIOT MONOPLANE ACCIDENTALLY LANDED AT BEXHILL 2/3/14 No.8.
PHOTO CHAPMAN. BEXHILL.

A wonderful shot by Chapman of Bexhill of a Hupmobile tourer parked beside a Bleriot monoplane which has accidentally landed there on 2 March 1914.

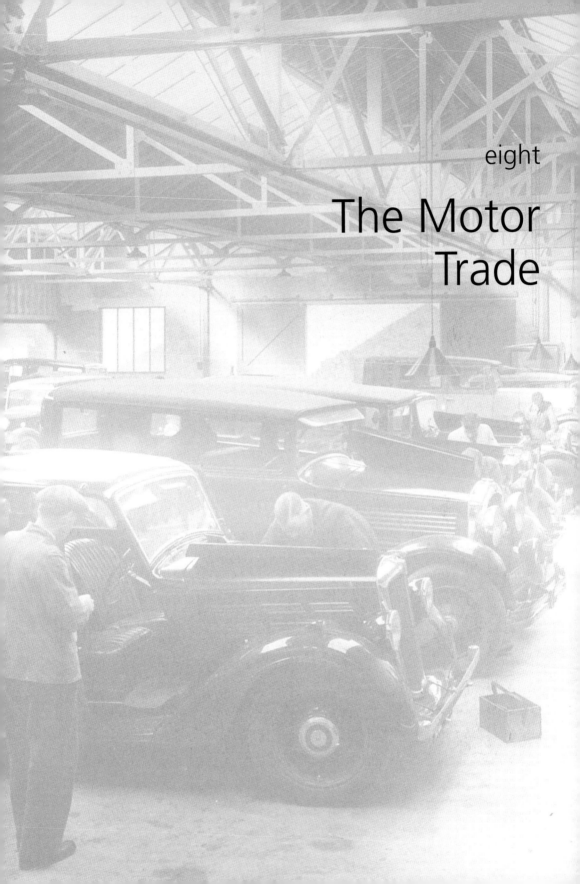

eight

The Motor Trade

The well-known Horsham firm of Rice Bros were initially coachbuilders and this photograph of around 1906 shows their staff lined up between two Panhard-Levassor cars. The right-hand car, BP 639, was registered to J. Rice on 11 July of that year, and was probably one of the cars for hire advertised on the hanging sign.

Particularly stylish are the premises of J.C.H. Martin in Cliffe High Street, Lewes, with two Enfield cars parked outside. The building, dating from the 1880s, was a shoe manufactory, to which Martin moved in 1904.

Brighton's Richmond Motor Garage is typical of many such establishments: the exterior is not impressive, but their fleet of hire-cars is well presented and smart. They are, from left to right: unknown, Enfield tourer and Th. Schneider 15.9. The garage was an agent for Belsize cars.

One tends to assume that a coachbuilder's premises would exude dignity and craftsmanship, but this posed photograph of the Brighton & Hove Motor Works definitely represents the rough end of the trade. In various states of completion are a Metallurgique, a Renault and a Straker-Squire, the latter presumably in for repair.

Above and below: The name of Mansfield will be associated by many with Vauxhall, for whom they were agents for many years. These photographs show firstly their showroom containing Ford Model Ts, and their up-market cousin the Lincoln, this being in the mid-1920s; and below a display of Hillmans in the same premises. This dates from about 1939, and features a 14hp saloon on the left, and Minx coupé and saloon on the right.

Tower Motors of Hastings display their fleet of hire cars adorned with flowers and white bows for a wedding, more tasteful and less distracting for the driver than the ribbons used today. Two Austin 20s flank a Crossley 25/30, all with landaulette bodies. Only the left-hand Austin is locally registered. Hiring was only one of Tower Motors' activities, and they were agents for Overland cars.

Caffyns has been a respected name in the world of motoring in Sussex from 1903 till the present day. This is an early (1904) photograph of their premises in The Colonnade, Eastbourne, their first location. The two brothers, H.B. and P.T. Caffyn stand between a Panhard Levassor and a Renault.

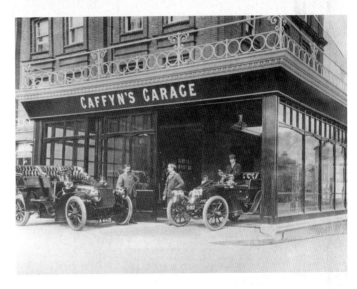

In 1912 the first branch outside Eastbourne was opened at High St, Heathfield, in this purpose-built garage. Seen here in the mid-1920s, the cars lined up include Singer, Wolseley, Essex, Clyno and Austin.

Above: The Uckfield branch of Caffyns was opened in 1934, in this distinctive building.
The showroom displays a Sunbeam-Talbot.

Below: The atmosphere of a busy pre-war workshop is well conveyed by this picture of Caffyns'
Dyke Road, Brighton premises.

Above and below: Caffyns were distinguished coach-builders, and some of their handiwork survives to this day. Here we see work in progress at Marine Parade, Eastbourne and below an example of their coachwork on a Mercedes chassis.

SHOOTING BRAKE
With Drop Curtains
SPECIAL DESIGN

Other titles published by Tempus

Motoring around Surrey
BRIAN GOODMAN

Surrey has enjoyed a wealth of variety of motor vehicles through the years. Here are images of big cars, little cars, townscapes, countryside and all sorts of period clothing to put it all in context. Over 200 images show a way of life the county will never see again.
07524 3260 6

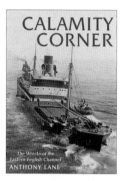

Calamity Corner
ANTHONY LANE

For over five centuries, the English Channel's eastern approaches have seen more shipwrecks than almost any other part of the coastline. Well known for its shifting sands, narrow sea lanes and rapidly changing weather patterns, Calamity Corner illustrates just how treacherous this stretch of coast can be.
07524 3163 3

Glorious Summer
JOHN WALLACE

Sussex CCC, established in 1839 and boasting many famous names over the years, had never been champions – at least, until 2003, when everything changed. This is the story of that glorious summer, told by long-time supporter John Wallace, making this book a must for all Sussex fans.
07524 3224 9

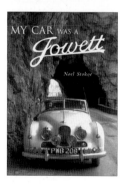

My Car was a Jowett
NOEL STOKOE

The Jowett was the only mass produced car to come out of Yorkshire. These Bradford-built cars were cheap and robust, and during the 1920s and 1930s brought car ownership to working people for the first time. Noel Stokoe has gathered together many people's memories of their time with one or more of these Bradford-built cars.
07524 2796 2

If you are interested in purchasing other books published by Tempus, or in case you have difficulty finding any Tempus books in your local bookshop, you can also place orders directly through our website

www.tempus-publishing.com